# If Found, Please Return To:

# VITAL INFORMATION

<table>
<tr><td colspan="3" align="center">Purchase Information</td></tr>
<tr><td>Year</td><td>Make</td><td>Model</td></tr>
<tr><td colspan="2">Date of Purchase</td><td>Mileage    VIN</td></tr>
<tr><td colspan="3">Purchased From</td></tr>
<tr><td colspan="3">Address</td></tr>
<tr><td>Phone</td><td colspan="2">Salesman (if applicable)</td></tr>
</table>

| Weight, Tow & Pressure | |
|---|---|
| GCVR | |
| GCWR | |
| Tongue | |
| Tow Capacity | |
| Tire Pressure | |
| Notes | |

| Tank Capacity | |
|---|---|
| Fresh | |
| Gray | |
| Gray | |
| Black | |
| Propane | |
| Notes | |

**Notes**

# MAINTENANCE CHECKLIST

Date _______________________________

_________________________________________

_________________________________________

| | |
|---|---|
| ○ Oil Change | ○ Water Heater |
| ○ Oil Filter | ○ Stove |
| ○ Air Filter | ○ Refrigerator |
| ○ Fuel Filter | ○ Furnace |
| ○ Fan Belts | ○ Fire Extinguisher |
| ○ Radiator Hose | ○ Slide Seals |
| ○ Water Pump | ○ Frame |
| ○ Fluid Levels | ○ Locks |
| ○ Chassis | ○ Latches |
| ○ Tires | ○ Trailer Brakes |
| ○ Wipers | ○ Exterior Lights |
| ○ A/C | ○ Interior Lights |
| ○ Lights | ○ Tow Coupler |
| ○ Battery | ○ Breakaway Switch |
| ○ Dump Valve | ○ _______________ |
| ○ Black Tank | ○ _______________ |
| ○ Gray Tank | ○ _______________ |
| ○ Window Seals | ○ _______________ |
| ○ Steps | ○ _______________ |
| ○ Converter | ○ _______________ |
| ○ Roof A/C | ○ _______________ |
| ○ Propane Tank | ○ _______________ |
| ○ Generator | ○ _______________ |
| ○ Fresh Water Tank | ○ _______________ |

# MAINTENANCE NOTES

# MAINTENANCE CHECKLIST

Date

| | |
|---|---|
| o Oil Change | o Water Heater |
| o Oil Filter | o Stove |
| o Air Filter | o Refrigerator |
| o Fuel Filter | o Furnace |
| o Fan Belts | o Fire Extinguisher |
| o Radiator Hose | o Slide Seals |
| o Water Pump | o Frame |
| o Fluid Levels | o Locks |
| o Chassis | o Latches |
| o Tires | o Trailer Brakes |
| o Wipers | o Exterior Lights |
| o A/C | o Interior Lights |
| o Lights | o Tow Coupler |
| o Battery | o Breakaway Switch |
| o Dump Valve | o ______________ |
| o Black Tank | o ______________ |
| o Gray Tank | o ______________ |
| o Window Seals | o ______________ |
| o Steps | o ______________ |
| o Converter | o ______________ |
| o Roof A/C | o ______________ |
| o Propane Tank | o ______________ |
| o Generator | o ______________ |
| o Fresh Water Tank | o ______________ |

# MAINTENANCE NOTES

# MAINTENANCE CHECKLIST

Date

- ○ Oil Change
- ○ Oil Filter
- ○ Air Filter
- ○ Fuel Filter
- ○ Fan Belts
- ○ Radiator Hose
- ○ Water Pump
- ○ Fluid Levels
- ○ Chassis
- ○ Tires
- ○ Wipers
- ○ A/C
- ○ Lights
- ○ Battery
- ○ Dump Valve
- ○ Black Tank
- ○ Gray Tank
- ○ Window Seals
- ○ Steps
- ○ Converter
- ○ Roof A/C
- ○ Propane Tank
- ○ Generator
- ○ Fresh Water Tank

- ○ Water Heater
- ○ Stove
- ○ Refrigerator
- ○ Furnace
- ○ Fire Extinguisher
- ○ Slide Seals
- ○ Frame
- ○ Locks
- ○ Latches
- ○ Trailer Brakes
- ○ Exterior Lights
- ○ Interior Lights
- ○ Tow Coupler
- ○ Breakaway Switch
- ○ _______________
- ○ _______________
- ○ _______________
- ○ _______________
- ○ _______________
- ○ _______________
- ○ _______________
- ○ _______________
- ○ _______________
- ○ _______________

# MAINTENANCE NOTES

# MAINTENANCE CHECKLIST

Date ________________________

_____________________________

| | |
|---|---|
| ○ Oil Change | ○ Water Heater |
| ○ Oil Filter | ○ Stove |
| ○ Air Filter | ○ Refrigerator |
| ○ Fuel Filter | ○ Furnace |
| ○ Fan Belts | ○ Fire Extinguisher |
| ○ Radiator Hose | ○ Slide Seals |
| ○ Water Pump | ○ Frame |
| ○ Fluid Levels | ○ Locks |
| ○ Chassis | ○ Latches |
| ○ Tires | ○ Trailer Brakes |
| ○ Wipers | ○ Exterior Lights |
| ○ A/C | ○ Interior Lights |
| ○ Lights | ○ Tow Coupler |
| ○ Battery | ○ Breakaway Switch |
| ○ Dump Valve | ○ ________________ |
| ○ Black Tank | ○ ________________ |
| ○ Gray Tank | ○ ________________ |
| ○ Window Seals | ○ ________________ |
| ○ Steps | ○ ________________ |
| ○ Converter | ○ ________________ |
| ○ Roof A/C | ○ ________________ |
| ○ Propane Tank | ○ ________________ |
| ○ Generator | ○ ________________ |
| ○ Fresh Water Tank | ○ ________________ |

# MAINTENANCE NOTES

# MAINTENANCE CHECKLIST



| | |
|---|---|
| ○ Oil Change | ○ Water Heater |
| ○ Oil Filter | ○ Stove |
| ○ Air Filter | ○ Refrigerator |
| ○ Fuel Filter | ○ Furnace |
| ○ Fan Belts | ○ Fire Extinguisher |
| ○ Radiator Hose | ○ Slide Seals |
| ○ Water Pump | ○ Frame |
| ○ Fluid Levels | ○ Locks |
| ○ Chassis | ○ Latches |
| ○ Tires | ○ Trailer Brakes |
| ○ Wipers | ○ Exterior Lights |
| ○ A/C | ○ Interior Lights |
| ○ Lights | ○ Tow Coupler |
| ○ Battery | ○ Breakaway Switch |
| ○ Dump Valve | ○ _______________ |
| ○ Black Tank | ○ _______________ |
| ○ Gray Tank | ○ _______________ |
| ○ Window Seals | ○ _______________ |
| ○ Steps | ○ _______________ |
| ○ Converter | ○ _______________ |
| ○ Roof A/C | ○ _______________ |
| ○ Propane Tank | ○ _______________ |
| ○ Generator | ○ _______________ |
| ○ Fresh Water Tank | ○ _______________ |

# MAINTENANCE NOTES

# MAINTENANCE CHECKLIST

Date

| | |
|---|---|
| ○ Oil Change | ○ Water Heater |
| ○ Oil Filter | ○ Stove |
| ○ Air Filter | ○ Refrigerator |
| ○ Fuel Filter | ○ Furnace |
| ○ Fan Belts | ○ Fire Extinguisher |
| ○ Radiator Hose | ○ Slide Seals |
| ○ Water Pump | ○ Frame |
| ○ Fluid Levels | ○ Locks |
| ○ Chassis | ○ Latches |
| ○ Tires | ○ Trailer Brakes |
| ○ Wipers | ○ Exterior Lights |
| ○ A/C | ○ Interior Lights |
| ○ Lights | ○ Tow Coupler |
| ○ Battery | ○ Breakaway Switch |
| ○ Dump Valve | ○ ______________ |
| ○ Black Tank | ○ ______________ |
| ○ Gray Tank | ○ ______________ |
| ○ Window Seals | ○ ______________ |
| ○ Steps | ○ ______________ |
| ○ Converter | ○ ______________ |
| ○ Roof A/C | ○ ______________ |
| ○ Propane Tank | ○ ______________ |
| ○ Generator | ○ ______________ |
| ○ Fresh Water Tank | ○ ______________ |

# MAINTENANCE NOTES

# MAINTENANCE CHECKLIST

Date _______________________________________

_______________________________________

_______________________________________

- o Oil Change
- o Oil Filter
- o Air Filter
- o Fuel Filter
- o Fan Belts
- o Radiator Hose
- o Water Pump
- o Fluid Levels
- o Chassis
- o Tires
- o Wipers
- o A/C
- o Lights
- o Battery
- o Dump Valve
- o Black Tank
- o Gray Tank
- o Window Seals
- o Steps
- o Converter
- o Roof A/C
- o Propane Tank
- o Generator
- o Fresh Water Tank

- o Water Heater
- o Stove
- o Refrigerator
- o Furnace
- o Fire Extinguisher
- o Slide Seals
- o Frame
- o Locks
- o Latches
- o Trailer Brakes
- o Exterior Lights
- o Interior Lights
- o Tow Coupler
- o Breakaway Switch
- o _______________
- o _______________
- o _______________
- o _______________
- o _______________
- o _______________
- o _______________
- o _______________
- o _______________

# MAINTENANCE NOTES

# MAINTENANCE CHECKLIST

Date ___________________________________________

| | |
|---|---|
| o Oil Change | o Water Heater |
| o Oil Filter | o Stove |
| o Air Filter | o Refrigerator |
| o Fuel Filter | o Furnace |
| o Fan Belts | o Fire Extinguisher |
| o Radiator Hose | o Slide Seals |
| o Water Pump | o Frame |
| o Fluid Levels | o Locks |
| o Chassis | o Latches |
| o Tires | o Trailer Brakes |
| o Wipers | o Exterior Lights |
| o A/C | o Interior Lights |
| o Lights | o Tow Coupler |
| o Battery | o Breakaway Switch |
| o Dump Valve | o ___________ |
| o Black Tank | o ___________ |
| o Gray Tank | o ___________ |
| o Window Seals | o ___________ |
| o Steps | o ___________ |
| o Converter | o ___________ |
| o Roof A/C | o ___________ |
| o Propane Tank | o ___________ |
| o Generator | o ___________ |
| o Fresh Water Tank | o ___________ |

# MAINTENANCE NOTES

# MAINTENANCE CHECKLIST

Date ______________________________

- o Oil Change
- o Oil Filter
- o Air Filter
- o Fuel Filter
- o Fan Belts
- o Radiator Hose
- o Water Pump
- o Fluid Levels
- o Chassis
- o Tires
- o Wipers
- o A/C
- o Lights
- o Battery
- o Dump Valve
- o Black Tank
- o Gray Tank
- o Window Seals
- o Steps
- o Converter
- o Roof A/C
- o Propane Tank
- o Generator
- o Fresh Water Tank

- o Water Heater
- o Stove
- o Refrigerator
- o Furnace
- o Fire Extinguisher
- o Slide Seals
- o Frame
- o Locks
- o Latches
- o Trailer Brakes
- o Exterior Lights
- o Interior Lights
- o Tow Coupler
- o Breakaway Switch
- o ______________________
- o ______________________
- o ______________________
- o ______________________
- o ______________________
- o ______________________
- o ______________________
- o ______________________
- o ______________________
- o ______________________

# MAINTENANCE NOTES

# MAINTENANCE CHECKLIST



| | |
|---|---|
| ○ Oil Change | ○ Water Heater |
| ○ Oil Filter | ○ Stove |
| ○ Air Filter | ○ Refrigerator |
| ○ Fuel Filter | ○ Furnace |
| ○ Fan Belts | ○ Fire Extinguisher |
| ○ Radiator Hose | ○ Slide Seals |
| ○ Water Pump | ○ Frame |
| ○ Fluid Levels | ○ Locks |
| ○ Chassis | ○ Latches |
| ○ Tires | ○ Trailer Brakes |
| ○ Wipers | ○ Exterior Lights |
| ○ A/C | ○ Interior Lights |
| ○ Lights | ○ Tow Coupler |
| ○ Battery | ○ Breakaway Switch |
| ○ Dump Valve | ○ _______________ |
| ○ Black Tank | ○ _______________ |
| ○ Gray Tank | ○ _______________ |
| ○ Window Seals | ○ _______________ |
| ○ Steps | ○ _______________ |
| ○ Converter | ○ _______________ |
| ○ Roof A/C | ○ _______________ |
| ○ Propane Tank | ○ _______________ |
| ○ Generator | ○ _______________ |
| ○ Fresh Water Tank | ○ _______________ |

# MAINTENANCE NOTES

# TRIP LOG

## Reservation Information

Park Name

Address

Phone                Email

Confirmation #              Reservation Co. (KOA)

Check-In                    Check Out

Cancellation Policy              Cancellation Fee

50 amp      30 amp    Full HU    Water    Electric    No Util

Site #          Length          Width          Rate $

# OTHER NOTES

# TRIP CHECKLIST

- ○ Sheets
- ○ Sleeping Bag
- ○ Pillows
- ○ Towels
- ○ Wash Cloths
- ○ Paper Towels
- ○ Toilet Paper
- ○ Garbage Bags
- ○ Table Cloths
- ○ Plastic Utensils
- ○ Paper Plates
- ○ Napkins
- ○ Dish Soap
- ○ Foil
- ○ Plastic Wrap
- ○ Lighter/Matches
- ○ Batteries
- ○ Dustpan
- ○ Broom
- ○ Bug Spray
- ○ Candles
- ○ Cell Phone Charger
- ○ Medication
- ○ Sunscreen
- ○ Lip Balm

- ○ Cooking Utensils
- ○ Cooler
- ○ Ice
- ○ Rain Gear
- ○ __________________
- ○ __________________
- ○ __________________
- ○ __________________
- ○ __________________
- ○ __________________
- ○ __________________
- ○ __________________
- ○ __________________
- ○ __________________
- ○ __________________
- ○ __________________
- ○ __________________
- ○ __________________
- ○ __________________
- ○ __________________
- ○ __________________
- ○ __________________
- ○ __________________
- ○ __________________

# MEAL PLANNER

| | BREAKFAST | LUNCH | DINNER |
|---|---|---|---|
| DAY 1 | | | |
| DAY 2 | | | |
| DAY 3 | | | |
| DAY 4 | | | |
| DAY 5 | | | |
| DAY 6 | | | |
| DAY 7 | | | |

# GROCERY SHOPPING LIST

# TRIP MEMORIES

# TRIP PHOTOS

# TRIP LOG



Park Name

Address

Phone                    Email

Confirmation #                    Reservation Co. (KOA)

Check-In                    Check Out

Cancellation Policy                    Cancellation Fee

50 amp    30 amp    Full HU    Water    Electric    No Util

Site #        Length        Width        Rate $

# OTHER NOTES

# TRIP CHECKLIST

| | | | |
|---|---|---|---|
| ○ | Sheets | ○ | Cooking Utensils |
| ○ | Sleeping Bag | ○ | Cooler |
| ○ | Pillows | ○ | Ice |
| ○ | Towels | ○ | Rain Gear |
| ○ | Wash Cloths | ○ | _________________ |
| ○ | Paper Towels | ○ | _________________ |
| ○ | Toilet Paper | ○ | _________________ |
| ○ | Garbage Bags | ○ | _________________ |
| ○ | Table Cloths | ○ | _________________ |
| ○ | Plastic Utensils | ○ | _________________ |
| ○ | Paper Plates | ○ | _________________ |
| ○ | Napkins | ○ | _________________ |
| ○ | Dish Soap | ○ | _________________ |
| ○ | Foil | ○ | _________________ |
| ○ | Plastic Wrap | ○ | _________________ |
| ○ | Lighter/Matches | ○ | _________________ |
| ○ | Batteries | ○ | _________________ |
| ○ | Dustpan | ○ | _________________ |
| ○ | Broom | ○ | _________________ |
| ○ | Bug Spray | ○ | _________________ |
| ○ | Candles | ○ | _________________ |
| ○ | Cell Phone Charger | ○ | _________________ |
| ○ | Medication | ○ | _________________ |
| ○ | Sunscreen | ○ | _________________ |
| ○ | Lip Balm | ○ | _________________ |

# MEAL PLANNER

| | BREAKFAST | LUNCH | DINNER |
|---|---|---|---|
| DAY 1 | | | |
| DAY 2 | | | |
| DAY 3 | | | |
| DAY 4 | | | |
| DAY 5 | | | |
| DAY 6 | | | |
| DAY 7 | | | |

# GROCERY SHOPPING LIST

# TRIP MEMORIES

# TRIP PHOTOS

# TRIP LOG

## Reservation Information

Park Name

Address

Phone                    Email

Confirmation #                    Reservation Co. (KOA)

Check-In                    Check Out

Cancellation Policy                    Cancellation Fee

50 amp        30 amp        Full HU        Water        Electric        No Util

Site #        Length        Width        Rate $

# OTHER NOTES

# TRIP CHECKLIST

- ○ Sheets
- ○ Sleeping Bag
- ○ Pillows
- ○ Towels
- ○ Wash Cloths
- ○ Paper Towels
- ○ Toilet Paper
- ○ Garbage Bags
- ○ Table Cloths
- ○ Plastic Utensils
- ○ Paper Plates
- ○ Napkins
- ○ Dish Soap
- ○ Foil
- ○ Plastic Wrap
- ○ Lighter/Matches
- ○ Batteries
- ○ Dustpan
- ○ Broom
- ○ Bug Spray
- ○ Candles
- ○ Cell Phone Charger
- ○ Medication
- ○ Sunscreen
- ○ Lip Balm

- ○ Cooking Utensils
- ○ Cooler
- ○ Ice
- ○ Rain Gear
- ○ ______________________
- ○ ______________________
- ○ ______________________
- ○ ______________________
- ○ ______________________
- ○ ______________________
- ○ ______________________
- ○ ______________________
- ○ ______________________
- ○ ______________________
- ○ ______________________
- ○ ______________________
- ○ ______________________
- ○ ______________________
- ○ ______________________
- ○ ______________________
- ○ ______________________
- ○ ______________________
- ○ ______________________

# MEAL PLANNER

| | BREAKFAST | LUNCH | DINNER |
| --- | --- | --- | --- |
| DAY 1 | | | |
| DAY 2 | | | |
| DAY 3 | | | |
| DAY 4 | | | |
| DAY 5 | | | |
| DAY 6 | | | |
| DAY 7 | | | |

# GROCERY SHOPPING LIST

# TRIP MEMORIES

# TRIP PHOTOS

# TRIP LOG



Park Name

Address

Phone                    Email

Confirmation #                    Reservation Co. (KOA)

Check-In                    Check Out

Cancellation Policy                    Cancellation Fee

50 amp      30 amp      Full HU      Water      Electric      No Util

Site #          Length          Width          Rate $

# OTHER NOTES

# TRIP CHECKLIST

| | |
|---|---|
| o Sheets | o Cooking Utensils |
| o Sleeping Bag | o Cooler |
| o Pillows | o Ice |
| o Towels | o Rain Gear |
| o Wash Cloths | o __________ |
| o Paper Towels | o __________ |
| o Toilet Paper | o __________ |
| o Garbage Bags | o __________ |
| o Table Cloths | o __________ |
| o Plastic Utensils | o __________ |
| o Paper Plates | o __________ |
| o Napkins | o __________ |
| o Dish Soap | o __________ |
| o Foil | o __________ |
| o Plastic Wrap | o __________ |
| o Lighter/Matches | o __________ |
| o Batteries | o __________ |
| o Dustpan | o __________ |
| o Broom | o __________ |
| o Bug Spray | o __________ |
| o Candles | o __________ |
| o Cell Phone Charger | o __________ |
| o Medication | o __________ |
| o Sunscreen | o __________ |
| o Lip Balm | o __________ |

# MEAL PLANNER

| | BREAKFAST | LUNCH | DINNER |
|---|---|---|---|
| DAY 1 | | | |
| DAY 2 | | | |
| DAY 3 | | | |
| DAY 4 | | | |
| DAY 5 | | | |
| DAY 6 | | | |
| DAY 7 | | | |

# GROCERY SHOPPING LIST

# TRIP MEMORIES

# TRIP PHOTOS

# TRIP LOG

## Reservation Information

Park Name

Address

Phone         Email

Confirmation #        Reservation Co. (KOA)

Check-In        Check Out

Cancellation Policy        Cancellation Fee

50 amp     30 amp     Full HU     Water     Electric     No Util

Site #     Length     Width     Rate $

# OTHER NOTES

# TRIP CHECKLIST

- ○ Sheets
- ○ Sleeping Bag
- ○ Pillows
- ○ Towels
- ○ Wash Cloths
- ○ Paper Towels
- ○ Toilet Paper
- ○ Garbage Bags
- ○ Table Cloths
- ○ Plastic Utensils
- ○ Paper Plates
- ○ Napkins
- ○ Dish Soap
- ○ Foil
- ○ Plastic Wrap
- ○ Lighter/Matches
- ○ Batteries
- ○ Dustpan
- ○ Broom
- ○ Bug Spray
- ○ Candles
- ○ Cell Phone Charger
- ○ Medication
- ○ Sunscreen
- ○ Lip Balm

- ○ Cooking Utensils
- ○ Cooler
- ○ Ice
- ○ Rain Gear
- ○ _______________
- ○ _______________
- ○ _______________
- ○ _______________
- ○ _______________
- ○ _______________
- ○ _______________
- ○ _______________
- ○ _______________
- ○ _______________
- ○ _______________
- ○ _______________
- ○ _______________
- ○ _______________
- ○ _______________
- ○ _______________
- ○ _______________
- ○ _______________
- ○ _______________

# MEAL PLANNER

| | BREAKFAST | LUNCH | DINNER |
|---|---|---|---|
| DAY 1 | | | |
| DAY 2 | | | |
| DAY 3 | | | |
| DAY 4 | | | |
| DAY 5 | | | |
| DAY 6 | | | |
| DAY 7 | | | |

# GROCERY SHOPPING LIST

# TRIP MEMORIES

# TRIP PHOTOS

# TRIP LOG



## Reservation Information

Park Name

Address

Phone                    Email

Confirmation #                    Reservation Co. (KOA)

Check-In                    Check Out

Cancellation Policy                    Cancellation Fee

50 amp     30 amp     Full HU     Water     Electric     No Util

Site #          Length          Width          Rate $

# OTHER NOTES

# TRIP CHECKLIST

- ○ Sheets
- ○ Sleeping Bag
- ○ Pillows
- ○ Towels
- ○ Wash Cloths
- ○ Paper Towels
- ○ Toilet Paper
- ○ Garbage Bags
- ○ Table Cloths
- ○ Plastic Utensils
- ○ Paper Plates
- ○ Napkins
- ○ Dish Soap
- ○ Foil
- ○ Plastic Wrap
- ○ Lighter/Matches
- ○ Batteries
- ○ Dustpan
- ○ Broom
- ○ Bug Spray
- ○ Candles
- ○ Cell Phone Charger
- ○ Medication
- ○ Sunscreen
- ○ Lip Balm

- ○ Cooking Utensils
- ○ Cooler
- ○ Ice
- ○ Rain Gear
- ○ _______________
- ○ _______________
- ○ _______________
- ○ _______________
- ○ _______________
- ○ _______________
- ○ _______________
- ○ _______________
- ○ _______________
- ○ _______________
- ○ _______________
- ○ _______________
- ○ _______________
- ○ _______________
- ○ _______________
- ○ _______________
- ○ _______________
- ○ _______________

# MEAL PLANNER

| | BREAKFAST | LUNCH | DINNER |
|---|---|---|---|
| DAY 1 | | | |
| DAY 2 | | | |
| DAY 3 | | | |
| DAY 4 | | | |
| DAY 5 | | | |
| DAY 6 | | | |
| DAY 7 | | | |

# GROCERY SHOPPING LIST

# TRIP MEMORIES

# TRIP PHOTOS

# TRIP LOG

## Reservation Information

Park Name

Address

Phone                    Email

Confirmation #                    Reservation Co. (KOA)

Check-In                    Check Out

Cancellation Policy                    Cancellation Fee

50 amp     30 amp    Full HU    Water    Electric    No Util

Site #          Length          Width          Rate $

# OTHER NOTES

# TRIP CHECKLIST

| | |
|---|---|
| ○ Sheets | ○ Cooking Utensils |
| ○ Sleeping Bag | ○ Cooler |
| ○ Pillows | ○ Ice |
| ○ Towels | ○ Rain Gear |
| ○ Wash Cloths | ○ _________________ |
| ○ Paper Towels | ○ _________________ |
| ○ Toilet Paper | ○ _________________ |
| ○ Garbage Bags | ○ _________________ |
| ○ Table Cloths | ○ _________________ |
| ○ Plastic Utensils | ○ _________________ |
| ○ Paper Plates | ○ _________________ |
| ○ Napkins | ○ _________________ |
| ○ Dish Soap | ○ _________________ |
| ○ Foil | ○ _________________ |
| ○ Plastic Wrap | ○ _________________ |
| ○ Lighter/Matches | ○ _________________ |
| ○ Batteries | ○ _________________ |
| ○ Dustpan | ○ _________________ |
| ○ Broom | ○ _________________ |
| ○ Bug Spray | ○ _________________ |
| ○ Candles | ○ _________________ |
| ○ Cell Phone Charger | ○ _________________ |
| ○ Medication | ○ _________________ |
| ○ Sunscreen | ○ _________________ |
| ○ Lip Balm | ○ _________________ |

# MEAL PLANNER

| | BREAKFAST | LUNCH | DINNER |
| --- | --- | --- | --- |
| DAY 1 | | | |
| DAY 2 | | | |
| DAY 3 | | | |
| DAY 4 | | | |
| DAY 5 | | | |
| DAY 6 | | | |
| DAY 7 | | | |

# GROCERY SHOPPING LIST

# TRIP MEMORIES

# TRIP PHOTOS

# TRIP LOG

## Reservation Information

Park Name

Address

Phone                    Email

Confirmation #                    Reservation Co. (KOA)

Check-In                    Check Out

Cancellation Policy                    Cancellation Fee

50 amp        30 amp    Full HU    Water    Electric    No Util

Site #            Length            Width            Rate $

# OTHER NOTES

# TRIP CHECKLIST

| | |
|---|---|
| ○ Sheets | ○ Cooking Utensils |
| ○ Sleeping Bag | ○ Cooler |
| ○ Pillows | ○ Ice |
| ○ Towels | ○ Rain Gear |
| ○ Wash Cloths | ○ _______________ |
| ○ Paper Towels | ○ _______________ |
| ○ Toilet Paper | ○ _______________ |
| ○ Garbage Bags | ○ _______________ |
| ○ Table Cloths | ○ _______________ |
| ○ Plastic Utensils | ○ _______________ |
| ○ Paper Plates | ○ _______________ |
| ○ Napkins | ○ _______________ |
| ○ Dish Soap | ○ _______________ |
| ○ Foil | ○ _______________ |
| ○ Plastic Wrap | ○ _______________ |
| ○ Lighter/Matches | ○ _______________ |
| ○ Batteries | ○ _______________ |
| ○ Dustpan | ○ _______________ |
| ○ Broom | ○ _______________ |
| ○ Bug Spray | ○ _______________ |
| ○ Candles | ○ _______________ |
| ○ Cell Phone Charger | ○ _______________ |
| ○ Medication | ○ _______________ |
| ○ Sunscreen | ○ _______________ |
| ○ Lip Balm | ○ _______________ |

# MEAL PLANNER

|  | BREAKFAST | LUNCH | DINNER |
|---|---|---|---|
| DAY 1 |  |  |  |
| DAY 2 |  |  |  |
| DAY 3 |  |  |  |
| DAY 4 |  |  |  |
| DAY 5 |  |  |  |
| DAY 6 |  |  |  |
| DAY 7 |  |  |  |

# GROCERY SHOPPING LIST

# TRIP MEMORIES

# TRIP PHOTOS

# TRIP LOG

## Reservation Information

Park Name

Address

Phone                    Email

Confirmation #                    Reservation Co. (KOA)

Check-In                    Check Out

Cancellation Policy                    Cancellation Fee

50 amp     30 amp     Full HU     Water     Electric     No Util

Site #          Length          Width          Rate $

# OTHER NOTES

# TRIP CHECKLIST

| | |
|---|---|
| ○ Sheets | ○ Cooking Utensils |
| ○ Sleeping Bag | ○ Cooler |
| ○ Pillows | ○ Ice |
| ○ Towels | ○ Rain Gear |
| ○ Wash Cloths | ○ _________________ |
| ○ Paper Towels | ○ _________________ |
| ○ Toilet Paper | ○ _________________ |
| ○ Garbage Bags | ○ _________________ |
| ○ Table Cloths | ○ _________________ |
| ○ Plastic Utensils | ○ _________________ |
| ○ Paper Plates | ○ _________________ |
| ○ Napkins | ○ _________________ |
| ○ Dish Soap | ○ _________________ |
| ○ Foil | ○ _________________ |
| ○ Plastic Wrap | ○ _________________ |
| ○ Lighter/Matches | ○ _________________ |
| ○ Batteries | ○ _________________ |
| ○ Dustpan | ○ _________________ |
| ○ Broom | ○ _________________ |
| ○ Bug Spray | ○ _________________ |
| ○ Candles | ○ _________________ |
| ○ Cell Phone Charger | ○ _________________ |
| ○ Medication | ○ _________________ |
| ○ Sunscreen | ○ _________________ |
| ○ Lip Balm | ○ _________________ |

# MEAL PLANNER

| | BREAKFAST | LUNCH | DINNER |
|---|---|---|---|
| DAY 1 | | | |
| DAY 2 | | | |
| DAY 3 | | | |
| DAY 4 | | | |
| DAY 5 | | | |
| DAY 6 | | | |
| DAY 7 | | | |

# GROCERY SHOPPING LIST

# TRIP MEMORIES

# TRIP PHOTOS

# TRIP LOG

## Reservation Information

Park Name

Address

Phone                    Email

Confirmation #                    Reservation Co. (KOA)

Check-In                    Check Out

Cancellation Policy                    Cancellation Fee

50 amp     30 amp     Full HU     Water     Electric     No Util

Site #          Length          Width          Rate $

# OTHER NOTES

# TRIP CHECKLIST

- o Sheets
- o Sleeping Bag
- o Pillows
- o Towels
- o Wash Cloths
- o Paper Towels
- o Toilet Paper
- o Garbage Bags
- o Table Cloths
- o Plastic Utensils
- o Paper Plates
- o Napkins
- o Dish Soap
- o Foil
- o Plastic Wrap
- o Lighter/Matches
- o Batteries
- o Dustpan
- o Broom
- o Bug Spray
- o Candles
- o Cell Phone Charger
- o Medication
- o Sunscreen
- o Lip Balm

- o Cooking Utensils
- o Cooler
- o Ice
- o Rain Gear
- o __________________
- o __________________
- o __________________
- o __________________
- o __________________
- o __________________
- o __________________
- o __________________
- o __________________
- o __________________
- o __________________
- o __________________
- o __________________
- o __________________
- o __________________
- o __________________
- o __________________
- o __________________
- o __________________
- o __________________

# MEAL PLANNER

| | BREAKFAST | LUNCH | DINNER |
|---|---|---|---|
| DAY 1 | | | |
| DAY 2 | | | |
| DAY 3 | | | |
| DAY 4 | | | |
| DAY 5 | | | |
| DAY 6 | | | |
| DAY 7 | | | |

# GROCERY SHOPPING LIST

# TRIP MEMORIES

# TRIP PHOTOS

# TRIP LOG

## Reservation Information

Park Name

Address

Phone          Email

Confirmation #          Reservation Co. (KOA)

Check-In          Check Out

Cancellation Policy          Cancellation Fee

50 amp     30 amp     Full HU     Water     Electric     No Util

Site #     Length     Width     Rate $

# OTHER NOTES

# TRIP CHECKLIST

- o Sheets
- o Sleeping Bag
- o Pillows
- o Towels
- o Wash Cloths
- o Paper Towels
- o Toilet Paper
- o Garbage Bags
- o Table Cloths
- o Plastic Utensils
- o Paper Plates
- o Napkins
- o Dish Soap
- o Foil
- o Plastic Wrap
- o Lighter/Matches
- o Batteries
- o Dustpan
- o Broom
- o Bug Spray
- o Candles
- o Cell Phone Charger
- o Medication
- o Sunscreen
- o Lip Balm

- o Cooking Utensils
- o Cooler
- o Ice
- o Rain Gear
- o _______________
- o _______________
- o _______________
- o _______________
- o _______________
- o _______________
- o _______________
- o _______________
- o _______________
- o _______________
- o _______________
- o _______________
- o _______________
- o _______________
- o _______________
- o _______________
- o _______________
- o _______________
- o _______________
- o _______________

# MEAL PLANNER

| | BREAKFAST | LUNCH | DINNER |
|---|---|---|---|
| DAY 1 | | | |
| DAY 2 | | | |
| DAY 3 | | | |
| DAY 4 | | | |
| DAY 5 | | | |
| DAY 6 | | | |
| DAY 7 | | | |

# GROCERY SHOPPING LIST

# TRIP MEMORIES

# TRIP PHOTOS

# TRIP LOG

## Reservation Information

Park Name

Address

Phone                     Email

Confirmation #                     Reservation Co. (KOA)

Check-In                     Check Out

Cancellation Policy                     Cancellation Fee

50 amp     30 amp     Full HU     Water     Electric     No Util

Site #          Length          Width          Rate $

# OTHER NOTES

# TRIP CHECKLIST

- Sheets
- Sleeping Bag
- Pillows
- Towels
- Wash Cloths
- Paper Towels
- Toilet Paper
- Garbage Bags
- Table Cloths
- Plastic Utensils
- Paper Plates
- Napkins
- Dish Soap
- Foil
- Plastic Wrap
- Lighter/Matches
- Batteries
- Dustpan
- Broom
- Bug Spray
- Candles
- Cell Phone Charger
- Medication
- Sunscreen
- Lip Balm

- Cooking Utensils
- Cooler
- Ice
- Rain Gear
- _______________
- _______________
- _______________
- _______________
- _______________
- _______________
- _______________
- _______________
- _______________
- _______________
- _______________
- _______________
- _______________
- _______________
- _______________
- _______________
- _______________
- _______________
- _______________

# MEAL PLANNER

| | BREAKFAST | LUNCH | DINNER |
|---|---|---|---|
| DAY 1 | | | |
| DAY 2 | | | |
| DAY 3 | | | |
| DAY 4 | | | |
| DAY 5 | | | |
| DAY 6 | | | |
| DAY 7 | | | |

# GROCERY SHOPPING LIST

# TRIP MEMORIES

# TRIP PHOTOS

DATE:

DATE:

DATE:

DATE:

DATE: ___________________

DATE:

DATE:

DATE:

Date: _______________

DATE:

DATE: _______________

DATE: _______________

Date: ________________

Date: _______________

DATE: _______________

DATE:

Printed in Great Britain
by Amazon

32541211R00063